THE GOOD

AND

THE CLEVER

T0349600

THE GOOD AND THE CLEVER

BY

A. D. LINDSAY, C.B.E.

Master of Balliol College, Oxford

THE FOUNDERS' MEMORIAL LECTURE
GIRTON COLLEGE 1945

CAMBRIDGE

AT THE UNIVERSITY PRESS

1945

CAMBRIDGE
UNIVERSITY PRESS

University Printing House, Cambridge CB2 8BS, United Kingdom

Published in the United States of America by Cambridge University Press, New York

Cambridge University Press is part of the University of Cambridge.

It furthers the University's mission by disseminating knowledge in the pursuit of
education, learning and research at the highest international levels of excellence.

www.cambridge.org
Information on this title: www.cambridge.org/9781107639362

© Cambridge University Press 1945

This publication is in copyright. Subject to statutory exception
and to the provisions of relevant collective licensing agreements,
no reproduction of any part may take place without the written
permission of Cambridge University Press.

First published 1945
Re-issued 2014

A catalogue record for this publication is available from the British Library

ISBN 978-1-107-63936-2 Paperback

Cambridge University Press has no responsibility for the persistence or accuracy of
URLs for external or third-party internet websites referred to in this publication,
and does not guarantee that any content on such websites is, or will remain, accurate
or appropriate.

THE GOOD & THE CLEVER

I WISH to take, as it were for the text of what I have to say, those charming verses of Miss Wordsworth's, the first Principal of Lady Margaret Hall. A text, however familiar, is read at the beginning of the discourse, so I shall begin by reading the verses:

> If all the good people were clever,
>   And all clever people were good,
> The world would be nicer than ever
>   We thought that it possibly could.
>
> But somehow 'tis seldom or never
>   The two hit it off as they should,
> The good are so harsh to the clever,
>   The clever so rude to the good!
>
> So friends, let it be our endeavour
>   To make each by each understood;
> For few can be good like the clever,
>   Or clever, so well as the good.

I want to consider the old and familiar distinction, and the different views which have been taken of it, to try to show that nothing will make sense of it, except to acknowledge that goodness is in its own way as rational as cleverness, if not more so, and that that means there is a reason of the will as truly as there is a reason of the intellect, and finally when we see the distinction of the reason of the will from the reason of the intellect, and their complementary natures, we may see why, especially in the sort of world in which we are now living, few can be good like the clever, or clever so well as the good.

Let us begin with the Greeks. Aristotle knew that goodness and cleverness were not the same, and he marked the difference by saying that cleverness was a power which could work opposite ways—for good or for evil. It is the power of discovering and employing the means which lead to any end which happens to be in view, no account being taken of the morality of the end. Cleverness, that is, is what people nowadays call ethically neutral. That is, I imagine, the last word about it. It is well to remember that it was as being ethically neutral that Aristotle put it below the other intellectual virtues. For there are enthusiastic scientists and philosophers who use ethically neutral as a term of praise. I lately read the MS. of a scholar who purported to have discovered that if you read the genuine MSS. of Jeremy Bentham before they were bowdlerized by John Stuart Mill you would see what a remarkable fellow Bentham really was. On reading his account of the genuine Bentham I concluded that what faint gleams of sense I had once thought to exist in Bentham were due to John Stuart Mill. My author remonstrated. Did I not see that Bentham had been the first to see that all science was ethically neutral and that therefore a scientific ethic must also be ethically neutral? An illuminating remark, for it means that for Bentham goodness was only being sufficiently clever.

But while Aristotle understood cleverness, he never got

right the relation of goodness to thought. Consider how admirably, with that consummate common sense of his, he saw the elements which make up moral character. He knew that it started with habit and disciplined behaviour, something neither irrational nor wholly rational; he knew that to pass from the stage of the morality of habit to rational goodness there was needed an experience which he called friendship: he knew that moral insight involved the understanding of ends or purposes and that that was a different kind of understanding than that which showed itself in technical skill. Yet for all that it is difficult to read the *Ethics* without feeling that something is wanted to make all those insights click together, and that in the absence of that something Aristotle, like Plato, over-intellectualized goodness. He does not perhaps go so far as Plato and hold that only higher mathematicians can inherit the Kingdom of Heaven, but he does seem to believe that only superior persons, and certainly not women or slaves, can be good.

To knock all that nonsense on the head took the teaching of Judaism as to paths in which wayfaring men though fools should not err, and of Jesus that to enter the Kingdom of Heaven men had to become as little children, and then the indignant remonstrances of St Paul: 'For ye see your calling, brethren, how that not many wise men after the flesh, not many mighty, not many noble are called: but God hath chosen the foolish things of the world to confound the wise.'

The reaction of goodness against ethically neutral cleverness went indeed so far as to provoke the pleasant remark of St Gregory Nazianzen that the Kingdom of God is not necessarily confined to fools. Nevertheless, it ought to have been impossible for any future moral philosopher to have produced an ethical theory which did not find room for the supereminent goodness of the unlettered saint.

Let us consider for a moment the facts about simple goodness for which I submit that room has to be found in any moral theory. Of course everyone admits that there are differences in goodness and badness which are not differences in being learned and being unlearned. But it might be held that the goodness of the simple man was goodness produced by habituation, as I think Plato held, or that there were certain moral truths which were so obvious and immediate that everybody, however un-reflecting or ignorant, must perceive them. On either of those views the goodness of the simple man, however genuine, is of a low standard. Such a theory does not account for the unlearned saint, or for the fact that there are people who though neither learned nor clever are outstanding in effective goodness and moral insight. It may be put by saying that some people have a wisdom for life which is not got by learning or by cleverness. Perhaps I may be allowed to read what I have written about this elsewhere:

It is an old story that wisdom in conduct is not learnt from books or technical study, but from experience and character. We know what we mean when we talk of men or women of 'sound judgement' or of 'common sense'. We distinguish them from the expert whom we rather distrust. We should defend this attitude by saying that the expert is a specialist: that what is wanted for conduct is all-round experience of people and things. 'Sound judgement' or 'common sense' are not the products of ignorance. They are produced by experience of a certain kind, by responsibility, by a varied acquaintance with men and things and by an *all-round* experience. The expert or specialist on the other hand has probably paid for his expert knowledge by having had to undergo a long training which has removed him from the ordinary rough-and-tumble of life. He has probably not had to check his judgements by practical experience. He has perhaps not had to pay for his mistakes. He has never had to count the cost of them. He has become 'academic' in the bad sense of that term.

If we think about the men and women whose judgement on practical affairs and on conduct we respect, we should certainly agree that academic education did not seem to be very important in their production. We should say that some of them were learned and some not, some rich, some poor. They have no special training or accomplishment. That is why we contrast the one-sidedness of the expert with the good sense or common sense of the *ordinary* man and why democrats think that the proposals of the expert should be approved by the ordinary man.

There clearly is something in this, but we must be careful. 'Common sense', it is sometimes said, 'is one of the rarest of qualities.' The word 'common' is used in New England as a term of uncommon praise. It means, I think, much what the word 'plain' means in the north of England or Scotland. We were proud as children when someone described our mother as 'the plainest woman I have ever met', though we used the ambiguity of the remark as a weapon to tease her. 'Plain' meant, as I think 'common' means, that she took people as she found them, and entirely disregarded their external attributes, their rank or class or anything else. Such an attitude of mind, receptive and humble, is essential to the true understanding of men and of life. It is found in all sorts of people who may have no other particular accomplishments and are therefore regarded as ordinary. But in reality such people are neither common nor ordinary.

The Greeks never sufficiently distinguished the good and the clever because they did not distinguish between the social and the natural sciences and therefore did not conceive of any science as being ethically neutral. The Greeks thought throughout in terms of purpose. As men's actions are inspired and explained by their purposes, and as the difference of the rationality of their purposes, i.e. their comprehensiveness and all-embracingness, made the difference in the rationality or goodness of their actions, so for them the differences in the behaviour of natural objects were explained by the differences in the purposes which inspired them. Science, therefore, involving like goodness apprehension of ends or purposes was mixed up with goodness. The difficulty of the Greeks was to understand that the unlettered could be good, but, further, to understand how the appreciation of purpose could be so differentiated from the pull or drive of action that a man might know the good and not do it.

Modern science at the Renaissance threw overboard final purposes, and therefore made natural science ethically neutral. It is significant that while continued attempts to reduce the social sciences to the same condition as physics in this respect have always been resisted, no one in physics has proposed to restore final purposes there. It has been accepted that this separation of the physical sciences from final purposes, and therefore from consideration of good and bad, has had and continues to have enormous advantages. And notice the result on our subject. It means that cleverness became what it was not for Aristotle, respectable, as is evident if we call it technical ability. Technical ability as we know to our cost in these days is a 'power of opposites' and can serve the purposes of death as well as the purposes of life, and its independence gives it such a degree of power as it never had before.

But the Renaissance reaction in favour of cleverness, as St Paul's in favour of goodness, went too far, as is usual with such reactions. For a new conception of nature was introduced with the birth of the physical sciences. The conception of purpose was given up and its place taken by the conception of a machine. The distinctive nature of a machine's working is that the details of its action come entirely from the complication of its static parts. Its drive is an undifferentiated push or pull; at most a push *and* a pull.

When the prestige of the new sciences suggested to moral theorists that conduct should be explored on the lines of physics, the natural result was an assumption that the same pattern could be found in conduct as in physical phenomena. Theorists assumed a pull, an undifferentiated drive, the desire for pleasure; or a push and pull—aversion to pain and desire for pleasure. All variation in conduct comes from the static circumstances. All thinking about conduct is on this theory a study of existing circumstances in order to predict future circumstances as they will affect the push or the pull, the flight from pain and the pursuit of pleasure. As I have said, Bentham worked out this view systematically and deliberately. He produced a 'scientific' account of conduct at the cost of completely disregarding the facts. Aristotle says of some views, that no one could possibly hold them unless he were defending a thesis. That is surely true of Bentham's Utilitarianism, and few moralists have followed his view that goodness is nothing but cleverness. What has been much more common is the assumption that all the rationality which is observable in conduct is the rational appreciation of circumstances and a calculation of what will happen under certain circumstances, on the lines of the ordinary workings of the scientific intelligence. The drive which produces action may be of one kind or another, but the one thing which can be said about all the *drives* is that they are irrational. One kind of drive or emotion produces goodness, another badness. This is roughly the position expressed in the famous remark of Hume's that reason is and ought to be the slave of the passions.

This is quite consistent with holding that some passions are good and some are bad and that we ought to enslave our reason to the good ones. For this view does not say, as does Benthamism, that goodness just is cleverness. It recognizes the distinction between the two. It holds, like Aristotle, that cleverness is concerned only with means to ends. But unlike Aristotle it holds that reason can have nothing to do with ends themselves. These are determined by the passions, by forces which, however necessary to social life, are irrational. If then cleverness must follow the ends which goodness prescribes, and the clever do what the good tell them, they will still be free to despise the good whose authority they follow, and can continue to be rude to the good and to point out what fools the good are.

But we have to agree, on this view, that if we talk of rational or sensible or intelligent behaviour, we mean the rationality or the intelligence of the thinking which accompanied or preceded the action; not of the will or the motive or the drive to action or whatever we call it. In my judgement all such analyses of moral action fail to account for what I have called simple goodness. To their prevalence is largely due the present remoteness of most moral theory from anything which happens in real life.

The contrasted theory, for which I wish to say something, maintains that 'rational' is an adjective as legitimately applied to will as to the intellect, that we can will rationally or irrationally as we can think rationally or irrationally. There is rational action and rational thinking. The characteristics of rationality display themselves in both spheres. A man may be highly capable of rational action and not highly capable of rational thinking and, on the other hand, we are all familiar with the clever ass. It may perhaps be thought that these remarks are platitudinous. Indeed, they seem to me to be so, but I do not think many moral philosophers would accept them. If we are to take them seriously they will be seen to have some interesting implications both for theory and practice.

The great exponent of this view is, of course, Immanuel Kant, but Kant himself said he learned it from Rousseau. There are two interesting passages in which Kant acknowledges his debt to Rousseau. In the one he says that he had been apt to take great pride in his character of learned man and to think that because of his intellectual attainments he was a superior person. Rousseau put him right and restored his belief in the common man. To quote his own words: 'Rousseau put me right; this blinded prejudice disappeared. I learned to honour men, and I should regard myself as much more useless than a common labourer if I did not believe that my work could accomplish something of worth to all in restoring the rights of humanity.' Kant had the great advantage of being the child of parents to whom, simple people as they were, he never ceased to look up. To feel superior is an obvious temptation to young people who are much cleverer than their elders, but Rousseau put Kant right. He was put right about the significance of the simple goodness of unlettered men and women.

The second passage is perhaps more remarkable. For in that Kant brackets Newton and Rousseau as the two great pioneers of modern thought, Newton in physics and Rousseau in the understanding of conduct:

'Newton saw for the first time order and regularity combined with simplicity, where before him disorder and scattered diversity were discoverable, and since then the comets move in geometrical paths: Rousseau discovered for the first time, under the diversity of the forms assumed by humanity, the deeply hidden nature of man and the hidden law according to which anticipation is verified by observation.'

Rousseau is in bad odour to-day. He was a romantic and we are suffering from romanticism gone mad. He started the worship of the group, which led to Hegel and eventually to Hitler; and in any case he is supposed to be mystical, and muddled, unpractical and highfalutin. Dr Johnson would have had him whipped at a cart tail and, in the words of Mr Podsnap, he was very definitely not English.

But what Kant got from him was clear and true: (1) that the laws of conduct are quite different from the laws of physics and yet laws; the beginning of the long story of the understanding of what the Germans called the *geisteswissenschaften*, a story which is to lead to Dilthey; (2) the distinction between particular and general willing. This second distinction has nothing to do with the much-vexed and to my mind largely unprofitable question, whether a society or a group of any sort can be said to have a will. For it is a distinction of attitude in the willing of any one of us, our attitude in making up our mind what we are to do. We may think only of ourselves, or we may think of, have a regard to, feel concern for, care for, other people. Observe the kind of language in which we tend to describe the familiar attitude, how the words like regard, concern, are a blend of emotion and thinking. Or if you like, of action and cognition in undistinguishable union.

Further, notice that there is all the difference between

general or rational willing as understood by Rousseau and Kant and that absorption of the individual in the mass, the irrational and disastrous consequences of which we are now witnessing. General willing, as Kant understood Rousseau to mean the term, implies that we determine our will by the recognition that what we will has to take into account others besides ourselves. Because in such willing we are determined by a principle our will is so far rational. When it is impressed on us in infancy that 'we are not the only little boy or the only little girl in the world', and therefore cannot expect this or that, or must do this or that, the process of universalizing our will has begun. This is the essential process of moral education, as we all know. It is primarily an education of the will, an inculcation of an attitude, a way of behaving. It can only be done in a group or fellowship of some kind, a family or a school. This is the habituation which Aristotle rightly described as the necessary beginning of the good life.

We all, I think, know this. The importance of learning to be a member of a group is widely recognized, in the practice of English education in particular, whether in the family or at school. It is behind the emphasis on team spirit and 'playing the game', which has been made so much of in English education that superior people are rather ashamed of it. But I believe that it has gone wrong—when it has gone wrong—because it has never got into educational theory as it ought to have, because our theory has been slow to recognize that the will can become rationalized.

But education in and by means of a group has one

obvious defect. If the group is to be of any use as an education it must be small. Plato's attempt to make the whole city the one group, a single all-embracing family, was bound, Aristotle said, to produce only a watery friendship. Yet if a group is small, it will tend to be exclusive. A fellowship has a fine sound: a clique a bad one. All effective groups tend to be exclusive, to regard non-members as outsiders, as though the very process by which our wills are trained to behave in one way to members of our group tends to make us behave in the opposite way to non-members. Indeed, one means by which a group becomes united is common hatred or contempt of outsiders or other groups. The common tie in which what is common has, for content, only being superior to other people, is a very real tie; as Hitler has shown by his use of the Jews as a scapegoat on which to expend all the feelings of envy and dislike which it is forbidden us to turn on to members of the group.

The true universalization or rationalization of the will depends upon our learning to rise above this exclusiveness. It is here that Kant made his great advance on the teaching of Rousseau. Kant, it will be remembered, uses the word reason, whether speculative or practical, in a very special sense. Reason for him as compared with understanding is the faculty of the unconditioned, the absolute or the infinite. He shows in the first *Critique* that while in the sciences we work on assumptions, premises, which are taken for granted, we are yet compelled, by the same desire for universality which has brought consistency within our assumption, to go beyond our partial assumptions to complete universalization. The principle of the speculative reason is to break down the departmentalism of our special and several inquiries, though it is by that very departmentalism that we have got any distance at all in making our experience intelligible. Reason has the same part to play in the practical sphere, to make us go beyond the limitations of this or that group, though it is by the help of such groups that we have begun the process of rationalization of the will. In the famous words of Marcus Aurelius, 'The poet has said "Dear City of Cecrops", can'st thou not say, "Dear City of God"?' We do this by seeking out the principle by which in the group we have learnt to discipline our will and to regard others as ourselves. As we learn to see the common humanity showing through the accidental and finite differences in men we come to a practical recognition of human equality and learn to have a concern and regard for all mankind.

Is it not the mark of the really good man, above all the mark of the saint, to disregard all the outside trappings and accidental differences of man, to get at the real humanity behind which is infinite? The really good man may or may not be educated or learned or intellectual, but though he need not be clever he is not stupid. He has the imaginative power of putting himself in other people's places, the power of imaginative sympathy, and of going right past difference of rank and wealth and ability and all else and getting to the essential human being. Think of the description in Dostoievski's *Brothers Karamazov*, of how

Father Zossima dealt with all the various people who came to him. He, of course, was a saint, but as we read we recognize that he had in exceptional degree a power which all good men have in their degree; of awareness of infinite possibilities in human beings.

Mr Walter Lippmann in an interesting passage speaks of the 'primitive intuition from which the whole democratic view of life is derived' as a feeling of ultimate equality and fellowship with other creatures. There is no worldly sense in this feeling, for it is reasoned from the heart.

There you are, Sir, and there is your neighbour. You are better born than he, you are richer, you are stronger, you are handsomer, nay, you are better, wiser, kinder, more likeable; you have given more to your fellow-men and taken less than he. By any and every test of intelligence, of virtue, of usefulness, you are demonstrably a better man than he, and yet—absurd as it sounds—these differences do not matter, for the last part of him is untouchable, and incomparable and unique and universal. Either you feel this or you do not; when you do not feel it, the superiority that the world acknowledges seems like mountainous waves at sea; when you do feel it they are slight and impermanent ripples upon a vast ocean.

I take my stand with Mr Lippmann here, except that what Mr Lippmann calls an intuition, given to some and denied to others, seems to me the final lesson of that rationalization of the will which is goodness. We learn it in learning to act as if it were true.

Thus the imaginative sympathy of the good man gives him an understanding of his fellows which is denied to the clever. For such imaginative sympathy cannot be ethically neutral.

If then we agree that there is a rationality of the will as well as a rationality of the intellect, and that goodness is not mere irrational urge or emotion, does that end our discussion of the good and the clever? Obviously not. For the more we believe that the principles governing goodness and those governing cleverness are distinct, the more we have to consider how they are to work together. Otherwise we shall be where we began, with the good being so harsh to the clever and the clever so rude to the good. Both sides have been inclined to say that their side is autonomous and self-sufficient. Science when explaining phenomena is to be ethically neutral. From which it is inferred that there is a realm of action where moral considerations are irrelevant and only scientific ones count. Conversely, ethics, it is supposed, when considering what ought to be done, need the good will and nothing else. Hence there is a sphere of action where good intentions are enough. Let us consider this latter position. Both Rousseau and Kant seem to have thought that to know what we ought to do needed no more than the good will: that that was always sufficient in itself to tell us what our duty is. That is a natural attitude in a small group, in the kind of simple society in which we learn our first lessons in goodness. In a family, or a school, or a simple democratic community like a Swiss Commune, the technical problems involved in action are comparatively simple and familiar to all concerned. The problem is to ensure agreement and common will. What matters then is goodness and the small necessary amount of cleverness may almost be taken for granted.

In this complicated modern world the situation is very different. It is not enough to make the range of our good will universal, and to become conscious of our obligations to others beyond our familiar group. We are called on to act with many people of whom we have and can have no personal knowledge; the effect of our actions goes far beyond the circle of those we know. The kind of intuitive knowledge of people and their minds we can have in a small group fails us in these circumstances. If we are to realize our good will in practice, we have to study and understand scientifically what the effects of this or that action will be. Good will is no longer enough. If it is to effect what it wills, to avoid the frustrating or preventing its intentions by ignorance and misunderstanding, it must enlist science in its service. We have to learn to be both good and clever. Yet the principles of goodness and cleverness are so different that the combination is not easy.

The trouble is only partly that preoccupation with cleverness or willed goodness may cause people to suppose that we can get on with the one or the other alone. That of course does happen. We are continuously being presented with a one-sided preference for one or the other. Goodness and cleverness are, as I said, presented as alternative gospels, as though all that is needed is that we should be so good that we can dispense with cleverness, or be so clever that we can dispense with goodness. There are those who persist in thinking that all our problems are technical problems.

Marxism, for example, is often presented as its earlier opposite Benthamism was, as offering an arrangement of society so efficient and technically perfect that no goodness, no courage, no honesty, was needed to make it run perfectly. If men spend most of their time on technical problems, they may easily come to think that there are no problems but technical ones. In this scientific and technical age that is perhaps the commoner perversion. But we are also familiar with the reaction to it. The upholders of what is called by its devotees 'moral rearmament' sometimes talk as though goodness alone would solve all social problems, indeed all problems of any kind. These extravagances happily have a way of refuting themselves. There is a pleasant story of a Genevan banker, who, when pressed to follow his wife and daughter into that company which chose as its title 'The Oxford Groups', said firmly: 'Mon fils et moi—nous restons Cambridge.'

The opposite perversion which rules out moral questions is perhaps more persistent in theory, but so obviously impossible in practice, that its upholders refute it by their own lives. What is far more difficult than showing the insufficiency of either by itself, is to show how to combine goodness and cleverness and yet keep the integrity of the practical and the scientific reason. In the times in which we are now living, if we are to meet the demands that are made on us, we have to extend the range of our actions beyond the small circle of our personal acquaintance. We have to work through organizations and use all kinds of long-distance means of communication. It is perhaps the greatest gift of the scientific intellect to mankind that it pushes back the limits of our perceptual experience, and enables us to deal with things and people at a distance. Aristotle said that a city must not be too big for all the inhabitants to be reached by an orator's voice. Think what broadcasting has done to the range of voices! Our actions have become long range and our knowledge of the effect of our actions has become long range. Modern government would be quite impossible without the technical equipment and the knowledge which the scientific intellect provides. But the extension of range is bought at a certain price. Plato in his seventh letter says the trouble about most instruments of knowledge is that they will tell us of what sort a thing *is*, while its authentic individuality escapes us. Psychological classifications, case papers, and all the elaboration of card indices does help one to deal with people more effectively, but the most elaborate and scientific analysis misses out the authentic individual, just exactly what goodness should have the power of apprehending. If we only deal with people as specimens of this or that, sorted out in the most elaborate of ways and put on the most elaborate of card indices, can we retain that reverence for human personality as we meet it in ordinary men and women which is essential to any true service of our fellowmen? It is not enough to have a good will, a conviction that we are bound to serve mankind to the best of our ability, *and* a scientific method. Good and noble work has been done in that way, but not the best. For reverence and understanding of our fellows need practice and refreshment as much as does the exercise of the intelligence. It is not entirely an accident that Hitler was the man who most successfully applied the card-index method to mankind. It sounds all right to say that he applied his techniques to wrong ends and we ought to apply them to good ends; but these scientific techniques are techniques of managing men, and that is one of the most dangerous of trades.

I have been reading lately an article describing the history of case work, the application of scientific method to charity. The story begins with an account of one of the greatest of Victorian women, Octavia Hill. She was one of the most efficient and capable of women and at the same time, as anyone who knows the picture of her as Miss Clare in George Macdonald's novel, *The Vicar's Daughter*, will agree, she was a saint. Her contribution to the theory of case work was the conviction born of her long experience that power to help anyone in the best way depended upon direct knowledge of and friendship with the individual.

By knowledge of character more is meant than whether a man is a drunkard or a woman is dishonest; it means knowledge of the passions, hopes and history of people; where the temptation will touch them, what is the little scheme they have made of their lives, or would make, if they had encouragement; what training long-past phases of their lives may have afforded; how to move, touch, teach them. Our memories and our hopes are more truly factors of our lives than we remember.

Her success confronted her with the difficulty that it depended upon her constant faithful attention to countless details. 'Really', she said once, 'it would be a small cost in value to pay any sum however tremendous to be rid of the annoying small perpetual care, if the work could be done as well; but then it couldn't: it is only when the detail is managed on as great principles as the whole plan that a work becomes really good.' Octavia Hill showed in a rare degree how few can be good like the clever, or clever so well as the good. And to read the subsequent history of case work is to see how hard it is to remain human and personal without being sloppy and sentimental or to be efficient and scientific without being hard and inhuman.

Sandberg, in his *Life of Abraham Lincoln*, tells a remarkable story of how Lincoln regarded the stream of thousands who called at the White House, nicked its banisters, smoothed its door knobs and spoke their wants and errands. Holding the greatest of offices, overburdened with the war, he yet spent two long afternoons a week in listening to anyone who liked to come and talk to him.

Why should the President wear himself down meeting this incessant daily procession, this never-ending scramble, this series of faces, so many asking trifles that could be attended to elsewhere? Halpine asked that. In Halleck's office they had system, said Halpine. Nine cases out of ten were turned away from the General in Chief to bureaus and departments. Usually when it was explained that the General in Chief could do nothing for them they went away satisfied.

'Ah, yes!' said Lincoln to Halpine, gravely, almost dreamily, as though he had thought it over many a time. 'Ah, yes, such things do very well for your military people, with your arbitrary rule, and in your camps. But the office of President is essentially a civil one, and the affair is different. For myself, I feel, though the tax on my time is heavy, that no hours of my day are better employed than those which bring me again within the direct contact and atmosphere of the average of our whole people. Men moving only in an official circle are apt to become merely official—not to say arbitrary—in their ideas, and are apter, with each passing day, to forget that they only hold power in a representative capacity. Now this is all wrong. I go into these promiscuous receptions of all who claim to have business with me, twice each week, and every applicant for audience has to take his turn, as if waiting to be shaved in a barber's shop. Many of the matters brought to my notice are utterly frivolous, but others are of more or less importance and all serve to renew in me a clearer and more vivid image of that great popular assemblage out of which I sprang, and to which at the end of two years I must return.

'I tell you, Major'—he had been talking with half-shut eyes as if in soliloquy, but Halpine knew now it was more than a monologue—'I tell you that I call these receptions my *public opinion baths*—for I have little time to read the papers and gather public opinion that way; and though they may not be pleasant in all particulars, the effect, as a whole, is renovating and invigorating.'

And at this present time while we are still feeling the blow of the loss of Lincoln's greatest successor, I should like to record an impression. Soon after Mr Winant came to this country I happened to hear him expounding to a small group the aims and hopes of his chief. I came away feeling how remarkable an experience I had had, hearing the intentions of a man in a position of enormous power who yet wants to use that power for simple kindly ends. There was the President, clearly with the organizational mind of the modern American, backed with prodigious power, saying the world is full of hungry people—let's consider how best to feed them: and naked people—how to clothe them—and people who are ill—how to cure them: and people with starved and perverted minds—how to preach good news to them. How men in time to come will think of Franklin Roosevelt in comparison with Abraham Lincoln we cannot tell. That they will so canonize him is very unlikely. In many ways the two men were very different. But they had both a streak which made their enemies say that on occasion they were too clever by half: Abraham Lincoln was at times as clever a politician as was Franklin Roosevelt: but in both cleverness was put at the service of goodness. In both the elaboration of the means was not allowed to pervert the simplicity of the ends, and so both showed how,

> Few can be good like the clever,
> Or clever so well as the good.

What then does this all come to? Something like this. That if we examine what goodness involves, we shall find that it involves not so much any kind of awareness or cognition—though that of course cannot be excluded—as readiness to act in the light of a larger whole, that is with a will which is rational; its simplest form is action as a member of a community in which all count—a readiness which then enlarges itself into willing as a member of the kingdom of ends. (If the community stops short of this and claims itself to be the end, the good is perverted to evil.) And that is perhaps a good conclusion for an address on Founders' Day, for it implies that we learn goodness as members of a community devoted to something universal beyond itself, and that is surely what a College ought to be.

Lightning Source UK Ltd.
Milton Keynes UK
UKHW010816070421
381573UK00001B/69